# WHEN DECADES BECAME DAYS

## JAMES DEREK TATE

Copyright © 2018 by James Derek Tate

Please send inquiries to
**jamesderektate@alumni.princeton.edu**

All rights reserved. This book or any portion thereof may not be reproduced or used in any manner whatsoever without the express written permission of the author except for the use of brief quotations for book reviews.

First printing November 2018

ISBN: 9781718112339

To my wife, Erica.

# Table of Contents

Introduction ........................................................................................... 5

Chapter 1: Pre-September 2008: Decoupled Markets? ................... 11

Chapter 2: September 2008: The Fun Begins .................................. 17

Chapter 3: October 2008: This Sucker Could Go Down ............................ 36

Chapter 4: November 2008: Cliff Jumping ...................................... 51

Chapter 5: December 2008: Darkness before Dawn ....................... 64

Chapter 6: January · February · March 2009: The Triple Whammy ........... 73

Chapter 7: April 2009 · May 2009: Aftermath ................................. 87

Conclusion: Wisdom from a Bear Market ....................................... 95

# Introduction

The S&P 500 reached incredible new heights during October 2007. U.S. Treasury Secretary Hank Paulson declared that the economic expansion during 2005-2007 was the strongest economic expansion that he'd ever seen.[1] Less than a year later, all of the world turned upside down. Impossible bank failures, crazy stock market swings, massive corporate bankruptcies, and surging unemployment plagued America. In times of immense stress and change, decades happen in a matter of days.

Before the bankruptcy of Lehman Brothers and the rushed sale of Merrill Lynch, nearly all market participants were unaware of the true carnage that would soon metastasize through the economy. Most professional talking heads on CNBC and Bloomberg dismissed the notion of a market crash from the Bear Stearns fallout. Even by mid-2008, the S&P 500 was down only a

---

[1] https://www.npr.org/about/press/2007/030207.paulson.html

few percentage points in the year. I spent July 4th weekend watching Joey Chestnut beat Kobayashi. Signs from Thor Equities declared 2008 as the "Summer of Hope" for Coney Island. People packed the boardwalk. No significant slowdown was obvious, and the word recession was not a topic of conversation among the general public. The National Bureau of Economic Research later declared in November 2008 that a recession had started in December 2007.

For most of 2009, even the smartest investors believed that the rally after the March 2009 bottom was merely a bear market bounce. In hindsight, two articles still resonate with me from that month. The WSJ published a famous article titled "Dow 5000? There's a Case for It" on March 9, 2009 (the exact day of the bottom), and Reuters reported a huge options trade in XLI, the most liquid Industrial Sector ETF. No one knew the psychological bottom, and the speed at which the economy collapsed caught many off guard. I remember Disney stock hitting $15 one morning in February (it currently trades for $115), despite the franchise brands and theme park assets having a value greater than $20.

Investors were either betting on severe deflation or a new Great Depression.

Fast forward to today, and it's a completely different story. American equity markets have entered the longest rally on record (despite a few hiccups along the way). Just last year (2017), we witnessed the most tranquil stock market ever recorded. Judging from the business news, one would be forgiven for being fearless. Pundits say stock markets have no memory, so maybe that's a good thing. Without risk takers, the economy and stock markets would be static. Unfortunately, there have been bear markets in the past and there will be one in the future. Nothing, not even government meddling, can stop human psychology.

I entered Princeton at an auspicious time, in the fall of 2006. Nationwide economic growth was on fire. Housing prices surged. Investment banks handed out jobs like lollipops. Bankers shuttled to Nassau Inn and Robertson Hall to discuss markets and the excitement they felt from being a Master of the Universe. I witnessed very smart people drink the Kool-Aid because of the money. Professors spoke about the Great Moderation and the end of classic recessions.

I remember those days fondly, and I'm glad I took notes. My freshman roommates will remember the white board I kept in our main room to keep track of my stock picks. I'd record the date, ticker, and the price I bought or sold. My rationale was simple: If I recorded my mistakes and wins, I could learn to be a super investor. Most people come and go with markets, but the rare few who stay can potentially become rich beyond belief after witnessing the same events again and again. I experienced a true stock market panic at age 20 and learned at a relatively young age just how low asset prices can go (hint: absurdly low). This experience continues to benefit my investment career. As information has become commoditized, mastering the psychology of the markets and weighing future prospects of companies are more important than ever. The real money is made by "letting the winner run" and making large, concentrated bets on a particular asset. Bravery and conviction are requisites.

This journal chronicles much of my junior year at Princeton, from September 2008 to May 2009. It is peppered with news, anecdotes, emotions, and raw first-person perspective as it happened. The purpose of this memoir is to educate people both now and decades from now about how the Great Recession unfolded.

This book isn't about credit default swaps, subprime bonds, or any of that other jargon that caused this calamity. It's about a perspective from a 20-year old kid studying financial engineering at Princeton who became addicted to markets. I'm the guy that "made enough to buy a Mustang" trading the markets during one of the most volatile times on record.[2] The experience was a lot like watching the movie Twister, but instead of becoming a meteorologist I became a public equity investor.

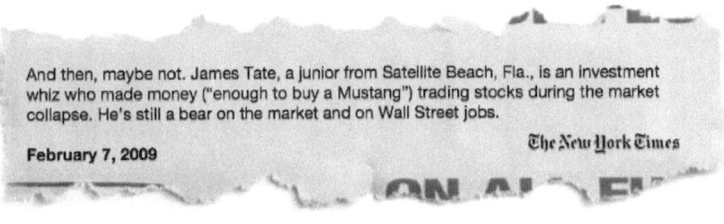

And then, maybe not. James Tate, a junior from Satellite Beach, Fla., is an investment whiz who made money ("enough to buy a Mustang") trading stocks during the market collapse. He's still a bear on the market and on Wall Street jobs.

February 7, 2009 — The New York Times

---

[2] https://www.nytimes.com/2009/02/08/nyregion/08towns.html

I take much inspiration from the late, great investor Barton Biggs who wrote *Hedgehogging*. Barton discussed the trials and tribulations of launching a hedge fund called Traxis Partners – despite having years of experience at Morgan Stanley – and inserted hilarious anecdotes about a day in the life of a 'hedgehog'. I recommend that book to anyone interested in markets or thinking of launching a hedge fund.

Let me also share the tools I used. Reuters and the Wall Street Journal were my main sources of information throughout the crisis. I religiously listened to Tom Keene and Ken Prewitt on Bloomberg Radio each morning from 6:30am to 8am. I paid for a special CNBC TV live stream (later discontinued in 2012 in favor of CNBC Pro). I also visited Firestone Library to read old microfiches of Wall Street Journal articles from 1907 and the 1930s.

Lastly, the chapters from September 2008 to May 2009 are written in diary format. In between certain entries you will see a group of periods (...). This denotes a separate thought process or subject within the same diary entry.

# Chapter 1

# Pre-September 2008: Decoupled Markets?

In the spring of 2008, investment banks scoured campus. The Nassau Inn hosted most recruiting events. Lehman Brothers historically hired tons of Princeton students every summer, and so many of my friends interned there before its enormous collapse. At one particular recruiting event, the head of Lehman Brothers investment banking expressed no concern about a housing bubble. They had just reported a fantastic quarter and saw the housing correction as temporary. I heard someone discussing Greenspan's "two lane economy": a slowing housing market coupled with robust risk asset prices.

JPMorgan had a major presentation a few days later where all the managing directors didn't speak much about the bank's practice areas, but instead focused on what they were buying with their large bonuses from 2007: Turkish real estate, a bungalow in Brazil, some hotel in Colorado. It was very enticing for most in the audience, but in hindsight just another warning sign. I spoke with one of these guys about his house half way across the world. This event was the first time I heard the term "decoupled" in the context of world growth.

The word "decoupled" gained traction, and I started hearing the word everywhere: major banks, some professors, and CNBC pundits trying to make a name for themselves. As the theory went, emerging markets were decoupled from the rest of the world – specifically US and European demand. Many thought emerging markets' status as net creditors would "bail out" other parts of the world, and that Chinese demand was primarily a domestic phenomenon. The Economist and New York Times wrote articles about the decoupling theory.[3] I think the growth of country

---

[3] https://www.economist.com/finance-and-economics/2008/03/06/the-decoupling-debate

specific ETFs and a weak dollar fueled the popularity of this term. The Great Recession later debunked the decoupling theory. Besides decoupling, the idea of BRICs (Brazil, Russia India, and China) propelling growth in emerging markets was all the rage at banking mixers. Jim O'Neill from Goldman Sachs became a household name. Many bankers said that global growth was the best since the late 1960s.

I spent the summer of 2008 interning at a prestigious boutique market-neutral hedge fund. The hedge fund community has always been an eccentric, money-focused crowd. Truth seekers gravitate to this edge of finance. During corporate access events (where investment banks will bring together investors and companies) around Manhattan that summer, many investors expressed some concern about a housing bubble. I remember visiting one IPO lunch where a "mad scientist" from Russia was trying to raise some money for a semiconductor business. Investors spent more time talking about the economy than the company. The IPO was pulled a few weeks later.

A market-neutral fund buys companies creating value and goes short (borrows shares to sell) companies destroying value. You sleep well at night because your portfolio is perfectly balanced. Anyway, while flipping through a Popular Science magazine, I came across an article about machine vision. At the time, there were a slew of competitors in the space and I selected Cognex as my area of focus for the summer. I won't say which way we bet, but my thesis played out correctly over the following six months. The founder of the fund where I interned, B, asked for me to come work during my winter break and re-join the firm the following summer. I accepted both offers. To this day, B remains the best investor I've ever met, and one of the smartest guys on this planet. More on the fund and founder later in the book, although both will remain anonymous to protect privacy.

The stock market is a measure of the status quo. The stock markets did not reflect true panic in the summer of 2008. From the perspective of a hedge fund intern, nobody was betting on the S&P 500 losing half its value nine months later. The average price target on the S&P 500 was roughly 1,600 on earnings of $100. The S&P Financials sector (JPMorgan, Bank of America, Morgan

Stanley, Lehman Brothers, etc.) was definitely weak and in a down trend – I remember Bank of America bobbing up and down and slowly going below $50 (the stock trades in the low $30s today after reaching record lows of $5) – but no one was suspecting what would unfold that fall. The founder of Greenlight Capital, David Einhorn, frequently appeared on CNBC about his economic views. Not many others were brave enough to speak their mind and voice concerns about the housing market.

One last point before the fun begins. I've always been fascinated by the 1920s. When I first learned about the Roaring Twenties as a kid, I was told about a very rich time in American history. President Calvin Coolidge ushered in a golden age of prosperity by lowering tax rates among the wealthy, and the stock market boomed. Jesse Livermore's novel *Reminiscences of a Stock Operator* depicts a very different world from today yet contributed a huge amount of knowledge about the markets from the early 1920s. I wish he expanded the book and included more years leading up to 1929. All we have from the Great Crash of 1929 period are old newspaper articles and old photographs. I think the period between 2003 – 2007 was very similar to the Roaring

Twenties. The Bush tax cuts led to a similar prosperity boom that the 1920s tax rate cuts had under Harding and Coolidge.

# Chapter 2

# September 2008: The Fun Begins

**Sunday, September 14, 2008**

**S&P 500:** 1,251.7 (Friday's Close)

Over the past several weeks, there have been rumors circling around Lehman Brothers. Choppy markets and warnings of potential systemic issues of the financial system are now rampant. It's a completely different environment than this past summer – way more sobering. Between August 1 and September 15, the mood in the markets has soured. When I turn on CNBC now, I sometimes hear doom and gloom. Fannie Mae and Freddie Mac were put into conservatorship about one week ago. A gentleman who covers the retail space keeps mentioning depression whenever he comes on the CNBC morning show Squawk Box. Host Mark Haines likes to calm him. People point to yield curve inversion as an issue. Yield curves have preceded all nine recessions since the 1950s; only one, in the mid-60s, did not. A Wharton professor was on Bloomberg Radio a few months ago and stated that he doesn't see any excesses in the country and the yield curve inversion may not matter anymore. The panic currently feels contained. By now, the idea of a mortgage meltdown isn't a fringe idea.

I'm mixed on what may unfold. Earlier in 2008, during my sophomore year, some of my professors spoke about Bear Stearns and the aftermath. All of them were adamant that the national housing softness was contained. I don't remember the Dot-com bubble or the early 2000s recession, but most people in the media suggest a future slowdown would resemble the early 2000s recession: hardly noticeable. Let's see if that becomes true.

...

Princeton's biannual Lawn Parties kicked off this morning to amazing weather and clear blue skies. I caught up with several friends who interned at Lehman Brothers and JPMorgan. Investment banking is the de jure internship for most Princeton people pursuing finance. Most of them seemed oblivious to the afternoon news unfolding. There was an "it will be fine" tone from friends. Everyone had offers to return next summer at their respective banks. I grimly joked a bit that all of these banks might go under, just like the end of the movie Fight Club. Several friends said they worked in "exotics" over the summer. Exotics, as defined by banking, sells structured financial products to sovereign wealth funds and pensions – in plain English: hard-to-understand investment products.

Very few interned at hedge funds over the summer, and I don't know anyone who interned as a prop trader. My core focus has been stock investing and learning about markets. I was taken under the wing of an amazing mentor and super investor last summer. I learned through major osmosis from B as I watched him think and invest. One thing that continues to resonate with me is how asset prices move. B has shown me that many times outside factors can influence asset prices, such as the overall market sentiment/mood. Then there's something called beta. Beta indicates the volatility of the company compared to the market as a whole. For example, if a company has a beta of a 1, then it moves with the market like

IBM or Exxon Mobil (although no company does this perfectly every single day because earnings and sector news also influence movement). If the S&P 500 moves up 1%, then generally IBM's shares move up 1%.

Clouding over this wonderful afternoon are headlines about AIG, Merrill Lynch, and Lehman Brothers. Reuters mentioned a few hours ago that Bank of America no longer wants to buy Lehman Brothers. Some are saying bankruptcy for Lehman. This bank survived the Great Depression and 9/11, but now might fail. I plan to follow the markets for a few more hours tonight.

A quick side story on Lehman Brothers. About a year ago, Lehman President and COO Joe Gregory gave an evening talk about investment banking and markets at Robertson Hall. Two of my close friends (we will call them D and J for the remainder of the book) accompanied me to this talk. I remember him discussing "taking ownership" as a banker: if the ink toner is low, get ink; if there is no paper, get paper; don't worry about asking permission. He also spoke about Lehman Brothers culture, at which point he walked around the room to take questions. Someone in the audience asked about mortgage difficulties (some kid in a red baseball cap, I remember). Joe said the mortgage difficulties would be surmountable. He said the toughest thing Lehman Brothers overcame was 9/11. A major portion of the firm was impacted when the Twin Towers fell. The surviving staff worked out of offices around the tri-state area, including a Holiday Inn in Jersey City. For several weeks on end, staff members re-organized the firm and brought it back from the brink. To Joe, the memory of 9/11 kept him on his feet.

...

This is an auspicious night for the Japanese market to be closed for holiday (September 15 is Respect for the Aged Day). Chaos now seems very real for US markets. I've tuned into Bloomberg TV and CNBC, and all sorts of people are calling in. There are topics I'm reading and hearing in the news that seem from a different era: potential nationalizations and bankruptcies of major banks. New York regulators and the Federal Reserve opened the derivatives market in a rare emergency session a few hours ago. I see a red-striped headline across CNBC.com and WSJ.com about a "Special Open Market Session" for ISDA members. Armed police officers are escorting New York Fed members around

Manhattan to meet with banking representatives right now. Here's a quote from the CEO of PIMCO speaking with Reuters:

> "This is an extremely, and I stress extremely, rare event. It also speaks to the more general notion that, in today's highly disrupted financial markets, the unthinkable is thinkable," said Mohamed El-Erian, the chief executive of Pimco, the world's biggest bond fund, based in Newport Beach, California.

The velocity of news has been insane all evening. AIG's credit rating just got downgraded tonight. S&P 500 futures are down about 3%. It's honestly hard to make sense of everything as it unfolds. Many times, market news never makes it to the general public until it's too late. Only catastrophic market events bleed over to the front pages. This day will be one for the history books.

### Monday, September 15, 2008

**S&P 500:** 1,192.7

Today is the official first day of classes. I'm taking four courses this semester: two from economics and two from financial engineering. I'm particularly excited about a course titled Money

& Banking. A lot of reviews pan the class, but it's going to be very relevant (I hope) this semester. After all, the largest bankruptcy in US history just happened hours ago!

Tom Keene and Ken Prewitt on Bloomberg Radio's *Bloomberg Surveillance* were discussing the events from last night. Interest rates were a topic. Some people think rates should be raised, while others think rates should be lowered. The financial system sits in a precarious state. Ben Bernanke, the head of the Federal Reserve, studied the Great Depression while a student. I trust that he will be able to navigate us out of this, but it won't be easy. Every single minute this morning the futures move down.

In the dining hall during breakfast, I spoke with some of the cafeteria cooks that I knew from last year. I asked them if they knew what happened last night. The guys all looked confused. They were speaking about the Eagles vs. Cowboys game and didn't have a clue about any bankruptcy.

...

There was a lot of dislocation in the market today. Oil prices collapsing 6%, the dollar surging, and the 10-year falling 25bps to

3.5%. Based on the commentary from CNBC tonight, some people think the market will snap back by December and that this is a "buy the dip" rally. I'm glad optimism is still out there. The Federal Reserve will have some announcements in a few days about recent corporate news. One gentleman stated that today's fall was the worst day for the Dow Jones since the markets reopened following the September 11 attacks. He cautioned we could see a year's long slide.

### Wednesday, September 17, 2008

**S&P 500:** 1,156.4

There was a short rally yesterday, with news that the Federal Reserve would hold rates steady at 2% and rumors AIG would be rescued. The markets closed marginally up from Monday, but today they tanked again. It's not clear what's happening. I see and hear two different things. My classmates, as per usual, don't seem concerned at all. I spoke with my economics professor, and he believed that the Federal Reserve will have to provide market liquidity if things got really bad. He thinks that unless investment banks really have been partaking in awful lending practices (which he says seems unlikely), then this convulsion in the markets will pass in a few months.

...

I believe that history rhymes. If we're going through a credit crisis, then this is nothing new. In the past 100 years, Western governments have experienced similar episodes of market panic. I plan to visit Firestone Library this weekend and go through microfiches from 1987, early 1970s, late 1920s, and 1932. I'm curious if I can gain any insight.

Also, the stock markets are super volatile right now. The VIX is in the 40s (a record), and the S&P 500 swung around 50 points today! It's unbelievable. Another interesting phenomenon: the US Dollar is strengthening. If a credit crisis originates from a country, then investors sell that country's currency. This is not happening with the dollar because of its reserve status. A big theme from the past 5-6 years has been dollar weakness and now it's unwinding.

## Saturday, September 20, 2008

**S&P 500:** 1,255.1 (Friday's Close)

What a week!!! No one had any idea on Monday that the markets would actually close up by the end of Friday. On Thursday, markets touched a low of 1,133.5 after news of Washington Mutual potentially going under and Morgan Stanley possibly acquiring Wachovia. Later in the day, markets digested news that major central banks would follow the Federal Reserve's plan to inject money in financial markets. The rally continued through Friday after rumors spread about a plan to relieve major investment banks of an impending credit crunch. 5-10% intraday moves on the S&P 500 is not normal! During the 1929-1932 period, it was very common for the S&P 500 to swing +/- 10%. Perhaps this is an ominous sign.

This afternoon, I did some digging on the 1987 crisis, and I found some very interesting articles. Kirk Kerkorian was interviewed about his views on the market immediately preceding the 20% drop in the S&P 500. He noted that if credit markets remained open then the markets should eventually recover in a few years and continue their upward trajectory. If the credit markets froze, then he expected a larger fall in asset prices. After reading a lot of articles from late 1987 and early 1988, most people from the financial and investment community believed that the 1987 crash was an aberration rather than the start of a prolonged bear market. I know credit markets and liquidity are important, but it's interesting how often these things were mentioned in these older articles.

...

Another fascinating development has occurred. The SEC plans to ban short selling of financial stocks. Any public company that has a financial subsidiary, arm, or business unit can apply. Ford, for example, will be banned. Here's some of the text of the SEC ban:

SECURITIES EXCHANGE ACT OF 1934
RELEASE NO. 34-58592 / September 18, 2008

EMERGENCY ORDER PURSUANT TO SECTION 12(k)(2) OF THE SECURITIES EXCHANGE ACT OF 1934 TAKING TEMPORARY ACTION TO RESPOND TO MARKET DEVELOPMENTS

Recent market conditions have made us concerned that short selling in the securities of a wider range of financial institutions may be causing sudden and excessive fluctuations of the prices of such securities in such a manner so as to threaten fair and orderly markets.

More can be read at
https://www.sec.gov/rules/other/2008/34-58592.pdf.

I'm not against short selling. I think short selling lets efficient markets discover the true value of an asset. In times of stress, however, short selling should be regulated. Markets, after all, are the intersection of fundamentals and sentiment. Sentiment can override fundamentals for years. Most traders can't separate emotions and markets, so they definitely will not in a market panic.

...

Famed investor Warren Buffett launched an offer for Constellation Energy the other day at a fire sale price. Lehman Brothers and Constellation Energy were trading partners, but now Constellation needs a lifeline. Buffett has been known to be patient. He finally got his chance to pounce. Constellation Energy's stock has fallen more than 50% in the past few weeks.

...

I walked around Nassau Street, but didn't notice a single thing that was different from last weekend. The weather was great, and the restaurants were full. I don't think the market chaos has spilled over into the real world, yet. My two closest friends, D and J, are concerned about the banking crisis leading to less job opportunities for next summer. We don't know if investment banks will slow hiring for next summer, but there are less jobs. Two large employers, Bear Stearns and Lehman Brothers, are now dead and there are rumors in the news that Wachovia and Morgan Stanley may go bankrupt.

## Monday, September 22, 2008

**S&P 500:** 1,207.1

$700 billion. Yes, you read that right, $700 billion!! Over the weekend, that number appeared as the amount of money that the Treasury Department will need from taxpayers. Something doesn't seem right. That's a big number. There are definitely better uses than propping up Wall Street. Why aren't average Americans furious? It's crazy. I would expect pitch forks and rioting by the end of the month... $700 billion out of thin air. I can't even reconcile that number because it's so enormous. One month ago the economy seemed like it would enter a temporary slowdown. Not anymore.

A previously unknown guy called Neel Kashkari is in charge of a program called TARP – Troubled Asset Relief Program. This program will allow the US government to buy toxic assets from financial institutions. My economics professor said in class today that he heard $700 billion was arbitrarily chosen, since $1 trillion would have been too big of a headline.

**Thursday, September 25, 2008**

**S&P 500:** 1,209.2

Crisis. Meltdown. Calamity. Panic. Credit Crunch. These are the five terms that I've been hearing as CNN starts to cover the unfolding market mayhem. Today will go down as the first official day that the general public will understand major issues are brewing on Wall Street. Last night, President Bush briefed

Americans during a prime time address about serious issues with the American economy.

My friends who aren't majoring in economics or financial engineering are beginning to talk about the market volatility. I've seen some signs for guest panels to discuss the ongoing calamity, and I will definitely be attending those in October.

A major source of debate at Princeton is whether or not taxpayer capital or private capital should be used for funding any bank liquidity challenges. Based on my understanding of 1929, credit was frozen. Instead of injecting liquidity, the Fed removed liquidity. It's most likely going to rest with the government to instill confidence back into financial markets. I'm drawing inspiration from other areas where progress was made, such as the EPA or NASA. Private capital always looks for risk-adjusted positive returns; public well-being is harder to quantify.

### Tuesday, September 30, 2008

**S&P 500:** 1,166.4

Market participants like to say, "The trend is your friend." Well the markets are certainly in a downward trajectory. September has been a wild month. Bloomberg Asia is currently on, and the month of October looks like the start of another bad month. Taiwan Semiconductor said that factory orders are weak. Yesterday, the Dow Jones suffered its worst point drop ever (although not percentage drop, the headline surely garners attention). Even after seeing a small rally from Monday to Tuesday in US markets, Asian markets look unwilling to follow through.

The pre-market has been much more active this month. I typically look at the S&P 500 e-minis around 8am, but the amount of activity from 6-8am is wild. I'm waking up earlier to see the action. I've now seen the major indices fluctuate several percent before the 9:30am open. John Silvia, chief economist at Wachovia (which just got sold to Citi at a fire sale price), said that credit markets remain very tight on Bloomberg radio. Credit tightness appears to be a major theme going forward, but one that seems anachronistic. I also learned a phrase called "Minksy Moment," which is a sudden collapse of asset prices caused by forced selling as investors race to cash. If it gets to that, I will be buying. The Depression didn't last forever, and neither will this period. So far, I've only been trading around the market. If the market rally from 2002 to 2007 lasted five years, a drawdown could last for a similar amount of time.

...

Another super important event: The TARP bill failed to pass the House while I was in my dorm room yesterday around 2pm. I remember saying out loud "Wow!" The huge plan that our President, George W. Bush, laid out is now in shambles. There's no floor to the debt market currently. Some people wrote on random blogs that Treasury Secretary Hank Paulson got on his knees and begged the Senate Banking Committee to pass TARP. According to Secretary Paulson, without TARP our economy faces a reality worse than most Americans have ever experienced. Outside my window, it felt like just another typical fall day. No one looked alarmed or realized what just happened.

# September 2008 Summary

- The bear market has arrived with intense asset price volatility. The VIX (volatility index) surged to the 40-50 range, which compares to similar crises such as the Russian default in 1998 and the September 11 attacks. Oil posted its biggest one-day gain in history on September 22, 2008. The S&P 500 dropped 15% this month.

- The average person hasn't noticed anything crazy in the "real" world unless they are looking at their 401(k)s. I suppose the first few months of the 1929 Great Crash played out similarly. Right now, panic is mostly confined to Wall Street.

- Presidential candidates Barack Obama and John McCain both appear out of touch with the current economic situation. McCain recently mentioned that the economy was strong a few weeks ago. [4]

- Market pundits are confused on the future direction of the market. Some predict it will rally wildly back once the government steps in. Others are less sanguine.

---

[4] https://www.nytimes.com/2008/09/17/world/americas/17iht-mccain.4.16251777.html

# Chapter 3

# October 2008: This Sucker Could Go Down

**Friday, October 3, 2008**

**S&P 500:** 1,099.2

As I write today's entry, I can't help but mention the carnage unfolding in financial markets around the world. While I've solely focused on US markets, the rest of the Western countries have also gotten shellacked. European governments are studying the situation, and several European banks like Credit Suisse, Deutsche Bank, Barclays, and Royal Bank of Scotland (RBS) are calling for help. At the start of this year, RBS was the world's largest bank. I'm not sure if that statistic still holds, but it is fascinating.

Remember an earlier hypothesis about the emerging world bailing out the developed world? Well, it's definitely not happening. US and European markets are falling just as fast as emerging markets. All these "experts" in the media and business community have been so wrong during this market selloff. I like to listen to people with public investment records, but very few spend time with the media. When Paul Tudor Jones or Warren Buffett speaks, every market participant should listen. Both of these individuals never publicly disclosed their view on emerging vs. developed, so we will never know.

...

Australian and New Zealand markets are getting pummeled with their US and European cousins, but their economies have been able to weather 2008 much better. I met an Australian banker this past summer, and he mentioned that US banks hawked awful subprime bonds to Europe and Japan. On their way out of Japan, they had no more inventory and so Australian and New Zealand banks avoided buying these products. Lucky, I say.

Wells Fargo decided to launch a stock buyout offer for Wachovia. Previously, Citi wanted a few parts of the business. The

Fed will backstop any crazy losses that Wells Fargo may incur on this purchase. Wachovia is currently a penny stock today (hard to believe). On the topic of Wells Fargo, I have a classmate who had an uncle recently get let go from its mortgage department after working there for 20 years.

…

During the Dot-com bubble, systematically important institutions did not fail like I am witnessing right now. Since last week, more and more classmates have been discussing the ongoing financial crisis. I think Bush's speech magnified what's going on (he's been quoted as saying if the government can't unfreeze credit than this sucker is going down), and now McCain and Obama are also discussing the economy during campaign rallies. Friends who do not follow markets are concerned about the financial system. Rumors are spreading about all sorts of other large banks that may fail. It's a scary time…Probably the scariest moment in markets since the 1930s. Professional investors now say October 2007 was the real start date of this entire calamity, when the market peaked, but I disagree. This feels more like revisionist history. Small fires smolder from time to time without spillover to the Dow Jones

Industrial Average. What I'm witnessing now is a once-in-a-generation moment.

...

TARP finally passed after a few revisions were made to the bill. I'm curious if next week the market rallies or fades. Yesterday, a professor asked for a show of hands if any of us are aware of the market meltdown. About half the class raised them, which shocked me.

**Tuesday, October 7, 2008**

**S&P 500:** 996.2

I attended a talk on FAS 157 and how it may affect the ongoing financial crisis. The Financial Accounting Standards Board, an organization that oversees accounting principles, introduced FAS 157 as a way for investment funds and public companies to value financial assets. It introduced a three-level hierarchy for asset valuation. In certain situations, some opaque assets may be worth less under this new rule than previously thought (mortgage bonds, for example). Rather than use purchase price, a financial asset must be marked to market. According to this lecture, many subprime bonds rarely trade on secondary markets and may be marked on a balance sheet at an absurdly low price. This markdown could lead to a vicious cycle of assets declining below liabilities. A chart of the ABX Index, which tracks subprime mortgage bond prices, appeared on the projector. An argument was made that the decline in the index has been amplified by FAS 157.

I'm not sure where I stand on the accounting rule. Any time new rules are introduced, people on both sides argue about them. The status quo can make up stuff about why the old ways work better.

**Friday, October 10, 2008**

**S&P 500:** 899.2

All the rage this morning has been about the US market's most volatile week on record. The Nasdaq dropped 15% and the S&P 500 dropped 18%. Going down with it was corporate grade debt. LQD, one of the most liquid investment grade debt ETFs, fell dramatically. A few classes discussed Pepsi bonds at 85 cents on the dollar. If Pepsi is going out of business, then there are much larger issues for society than a bad bond price. We're talking about major unemployment and a societal meltdown.

During my lunchtime, I was watching CNBC and witnessed another incredible piece of history. Congressman Barney Frank stormed out of a room and walked right past television cameras. There are rumors that Morgan Stanley may be nationalized. As I write this, the stock is hitting all-time lows at $7! The chart literally looks like it's falling straight down. I consider Goldman Sachs and Morgan Stanley to be the two premier investment banking brands. I'm shocked right now, yet I look outside the courtyard in Holder Hall, and it's a nice sunny day. Lots of other students walking to class with no inkling of panic. Several times during this crisis, the real world and the "market world" feel disconnected... This is another one of those times.

...

The Wall Street Journal had an interesting article about the week's volatility. So many people are reporting about the unprecedented market conditions. I thought this quote was fascinating:

Mr. Baer, who was a Treasury-futures trader on the floor of the Chicago Board of Trade in 1987, said, "I've never seen a credit market like this one. The fear has gotten way ahead of the fundamentals," including an unprecedented round of coordinated central-bank rate cuts this week that would normally prompt banks to increase their lending to one another.[5]

**Monday, October 13, 2008**

**S&P 500:** 1,003.4

Over the weekend, financial news reporters spent time discussing Richard "Dick" Fuld's Congressional Hearing. Richard Fuld was the Chairman and CEO of Lehman Brothers. A single picture, which I think will go into history books, shows Fuld standing in front of pink handwritten signs with the words Greed and Shame on them. The seriousness of Fuld's face captures the moment. I've mentioned that Lehman Brothers was a big feeder for Princeton students. Last year, an internal video on YouTube circulated with Dick Fuld talking about squeezing shorts. It's hilarious, and I'll remind myself here to view it again years from now. I can really feel the confidence from him.

---

[5] https://www.wsj.com/articles/SB122363315976122397

One thing I've noticed this fall is the amount of crisp sunny days at Princeton. Sometimes good weather in New York means an up day for the markets, but that trend hasn't held during this market downturn. The S&P 500 has swung hundreds of points up and down on sunny days. I pulled up a list of most volatile intraday swings, and they are from the 1929-1932 period and now 2008. Unbelievable! These are absolutely, positively the choppiest markets any living trader has ever seen.

…

It's been about one month since Lehman Brothers filed for bankruptcy. Thirty days goes by very quickly, but all the "experts" are unsure which direction the economy and financial markets are headed. Nobody knows. The government fortunately took quick, decisive action weeks ago (and more action continues). Despite all the flack that Bernanke, Geithner, and Paulson are receiving, they are the leaders we need in a time such as this. Europe continues to dilly dally because of potential ramifications, while the USA implemented a toxic asset disposal program earlier this month.

### Wednesday, October 15, 2008

**S&P 500:** 907.8

The investment grade debt markets are getting destroyed. Quality companies like Pepsi and 3M are seeing bonds move into the 80c and 90c range. If companies like this go under, society will have a much larger problem than a busted stock market. We've been discussing in a financial engineering class about the unfolding credit crunch. The big word floating around today is Depression. If TARP fails, most pundits on CNBC and Bloomberg think a Depression (yes, capital D) will happen. Just a few weeks ago, there were glimmers of hope but today the mood is very, very somber. A teaching assistant lived through the Russian economic collapse in the mid-1990s. He told me if we go through the same thing, we all better hope there is a God. Yikes.

### Monday, October 20, 2008

**S&P 500:** 985.4

I have been day trading the market as volatility has increased. Swings that would take a week or a month can now happen in an hour. Stocks charts only capture the closing price, so years from now people won't be able to see how volatile October 2008 really was. Morgan Stanley, for example, doesn't show the $7 intra-day movement – only the closing price close to $10. I've brought this up frequently in classroom discussions while we're debating how historians will chronicle the period. I do not believe that anyone can capture the roller coaster of the market, complete with the human emotions.

...

Bad news is an investor's best friend. Warren Buffet wrote an op-ed in the New York Times last week about how he's started buying stocks. He wrote about how markets have always pulled ahead despite wars, recessions, and politics. Based on Buffett's history, he's probably correct. The average American, unfortunately, doesn't read the New York Times and won't understand the gravity of Buffett's words.

### Thursday, October 23, 2008

**S&P 500:** 908.1

The panic is real and it's tremendous. I cannot overstate how much chaos grips the market. From Monday's close to today, the market has dropped about 100 points. If we continue at this rate, then the entire S&P 500 will reach zero in nine more days. On Bloomberg this morning, a few market pundits are discussing money inflows into the market. Apparently, money that previously left the market last month is beginning to wade back in. Whether this means anything, I don't know. If a bull market can last several years, so can a bear market. People always want quick answers in today's world, but market chaos takes a long time to settle down.

...

One of my professors mentioned he sold his multimillion-dollar stock portfolio. He examined the periods in 1929 and 1972 and decided that the market might fall another 40-50%. That would bring the S&P 500 to about 450. Classical valuations, such as the P/E ratio, are hard to measure because the future outlook of the economy has become so negative and murky. While the word Depression floated around a week ago, the word deflation has gained traction. If prices are cheaper tomorrow than today, then people will stave off making purchases. Emotions have gotten the better part of a lot of smart people lately. I've read several important investing books in the past two years, and markets always move up over time like a step chart with large bumps along the way. I think 2008 will end up being one of those bumps. My understanding is that if markets go down too low, then future returns are higher.

### Saturday, October 25, 2008

**S&P 500:** 876.8 (Friday's Close)

B called me today to discuss some ideas around Electronic Arts. I'm going to do some work on their recent game release slate. We also spoke about ongoing turmoil in the markets and agreed that a potential depression may be around the corner. Historically, an 85% decline in markets marked the bottoms of economic collapses. That would bring the S&P 500 to about 250, but with government intervention/TARP it may be unrealistic. There will be a time to profit greatly, he said. For now, it's best to sit tight and watch it all play out. B sleeps well at night because he runs a market-neutral fund, so emotions haven't taken control of his mind. He still has clarity of thought.

Ken Griffin of Citadel hosted a special conference call last night and B listened to it. Griffin wanted to assure investors that his hedge fund was fine, and that volatility will pass soon. A lot of hedge funds are getting redemption requests, and Citadel could become another victim if everyone heads for the exits.

Contractions in the business cycle were once all labeled depressions. When the early 1930s had a "great" depression, future government officials labeled slowdowns as recessions because the word depression had gained so much notoriety. I'm beginning to wonder what might replace the word recession.

# October 2008 Summary

- America's financial markets appear to be destroying themselves. Potential nationalizations of major financial institutions inject further chaos into the stock market. The speed of October's selloff surprises several prominent investors and economists.

- Google Trends reports that depression and deflation are two of the most popular words searched during the month. The VIX surges to record highs.

- The carnage in Middle America is real. People are losing their livelihoods as growth halts and the economy contracts. Yet, history shows again and again that these moments are the best periods to start buying risk assets.

- Investment grade credit markets hit Armageddon lows earlier in the month but recover as the month progresses.

Congress is discussing other relief programs besides TARP.

- Investment legend Warren Buffett starts buying equities.[6]

---

[6] https://www.nytimes.com/2008/10/17/opinion/17buffett.html

# Chapter 4

# November 2008: Cliff Jumping

**Tuesday, November 4, 2008**

**S&P 500:** 1,005.8

The rearview mirror of this market looks horrendous. When I pull up a chart, the S&P 500 resembles a steep cliff. News about the future of the economy can be disorienting right now. There are radicals on both sides of the spectrum, but CNBC has given air time to a lot of the doomsayers. I have read about market cycles and human psychology. Human brains don't process information well in times of stress. Add in money, and the current trauma is a toxic cocktail of irrational investor behavior.

Over the past two years at Princeton, I have been taught dozens of ways to measure the value of a risk asset. All of these equations have since broken down in today's deflationary environment. Behavioral economics is a new field of study, but it is not part of our curriculum. Sentiment and fundamentals are the two components to any investment, whether it's a bond, stock, or piece of real estate. They interact and compete at various times. While the future outlook for earnings gets murkier by the day, not all selling can be attributed to poor business fundamentals. A lot of investors don't understand that, so stocks are overshooting to the downside.

...

Today is election day, and Obama remains the clear favorite. There is a certain amount of energy and excitement that surrounds his campaign, especially from young voters. Investors are fearful that Obama will spread a socialist agenda. I viewed a video on YouTube a few weeks ago where he discussed company margins as being "exploitative," but I think he would like companies to pay workers more. When Obama picked Joe Biden as his running mate, I became less concerned about him being a fringe candidate. I voted early last week in Florida and spoke with others waiting in ine about the economy. People are definitely anxious about the economy. A gentleman in front of me discussed how sudden the economy tanked and thinks it's a conspiracy to get a Democrat elected.

...

Update: Obama has officially won the election. In Asian trading, US stock futures are tanking.

**Wednesday, November 5, 2008**

**S&P 500:** 952.8

Just as expected: markets sold off today. Investors see a double whammy of sick economy and potentially socialist president (sadly, his race may be playing a subconscious factor). Obama has signaled he plans to maintain Bush's crisis-era framework as he takes office in January.

...

Once upon a time in 2006, markets felt solid. Today, they do not. The amount of volatility continues to astound me. During a bull market, there are periods of stress that end in minor corrections. When financial news covers the frontpage of major newspapers for consecutive days, such as the New York Times, and share volume vastly increases, then there is a real panic in the markets. I'm not calling for a market bottom yet because there are still plenty of unknown variables. The volatility index hasn't calmed down and the economy hasn't stopped declining. High yield spreads remain very wide. Historically, the time to buy markets is when the economy stops shrinking but that's only possible to know in hindsight. Everyone on CNBC and Bloomberg keeps talking about capitulation selling, yet I've witnessed several of these high-volume selloffs without seeing a finale. I don't believe in any divine signal that gives market participants an all-clear sign.

...

I continue to use the S&P 500 ETF, SPY, as my way to express views on the markets. I've had a lot of fun taking advantage of the bear market rallies, especially when stocks are moving 5-10% in a single day! I try to close out the position every couple days because the gyrations are nauseating.

**Monday, November 10, 2008**

**S&P 500:** 919.2

While walking with D (the close friend who I mentioned in the September chapter) along Prospect Avenue, I saw our own Noble prize-winning professor Paul Krugman. Cameramen were snapping photos as he walked down steps from Robertson Hall. I briefly asked him if he would buy stocks at these low levels and he said "Maybe". Nothing topped that interaction today.

**Thursday, November 13, 2008**

**S&P 500:** 911.3

This morning we're in the midst of a high-volume selloff. I'm also reading rumors of Saudi princes selling their entire stock portfolios. The amount of people exiting the market feels bottomless, but it can't go on forever. A great Wall Street Journal article is being discussed right now on CNBC. John H. Cochrane wrote a piece titled "Is Now the Time to Buy Stocks?" for yesterday's paper.[7] There are many elements of this current selloff that resemble forced selling because price movements are spastic and nonsensical many times. Up. Down. Upside Down. Here's a great excerpt from Cochrane's commentary:

---

[7] https://www.wsj.com/articles/SB122645226692719401

But as I read the news, the "risk aversion" story seems more plausible. We are in, or headed for, a recession. Anyone whose job or business will be impacted can't take stock-market risks, and should be selling despite low prices. We are seeing lots of "deleveraging," "disintermediation" and "forced selling." As losses mount, investors or institutions that have borrowed money must sell to avoid bankruptcy. Others, such as some university endowments or defined-benefit pension funds, have backstop commitments that must be honored, and they too must "capitulate" at some point. Still others may just be less willing to take risks after suffering a huge loss, a sensible "once burned, twice shy" mentality.

All of these actors become more averse to holding risks as the market declines, so they sell. This increasing risk aversion amplifies an initial price decline -- coming from bad earnings news or the huge rise in credit spreads -- into a rout.

I love this article. Neoclassical economics dismissed investor psychology over the past decade. In fact, I hope 2008 shatters an awful notion of the "rational" market participant – there aren't any. Every single person is unique. Cochrane's basic message to investors is that unless we truly fall into a deep depression, stocks right now are starting to offer attractive values. He views stocks as essentially very long-term bonds that never mature. There are two components to a stock's annual yield: the earnings yield and dividend yield. The higher the combined yield, the greater the future performance. He thinks emotions have gotten the best of people today because a sound mind would understand that. At 800-900 on the S&P 500, a base could be forming.

What started in mid-September as a pragmatic selloff has spiraled into a chaotic mosh pit. As of mid-November, the market trend remains firmly down. I plan to start wading into index funds over the next couple weeks because the government has developed some relief for investors in the form of something potentially called "quantitative easing." This is a brand-new term, but the Japanese pioneered it in the late 1990s. I like listening to the older investors who speak on Bloomberg Radio because they like to share a lot of insights from prior bear markets. These guys also are familiar with the tools at the Fed's disposal.

**Tuesday, November 18, 2008**

**S&P 500:** 859.1

Art Laffer has been a frequent guest on Tom Keene and Ken Prewitt's morning show on Bloomberg Radio. He created the famous Laffer curve during the Reagan administration. The conversation with him is very casual, which makes me think all three of the gentlemen are close friends. Most of the dialogue revolves around economic theory and future outlook for markets. They discussed last week's Congressional hearing with the top hedge fund managers in the country.

Our politicians think that some of the crisis has been made more acute by hedge funds. Five hedge fund managers – Philip A. Falcone, Kenneth C. Griffin, John Paulson. James Simons, and George Soros – were summoned to testify before Congress last week. Having worked in the hedge fund industry as an intern, I think the investment banks are the sole financial firms responsible for the crisis. Hedge funds don't create crappy mortgage bonds and sell them to unsuspecting buyers. There is a lot of misunderstanding and mudslinging in the press about anyone having anything to do with Wall Street. It makes complete sense. Congress has to look like they are interviewing all the known suspects.

...

Today in class we debated about fundamental market value and I was the sole guy who made a point about how markets can drive people crazy. I said that a successful investor must have extremely strong technical and financial skills as well as strong insights into psychological and social trends. That combination is rare. Stocks are overshooting to the downside right now and will continue to fall until the last seller is exhausted. No math equation can model human behavior, especially during an enormous bear market. People can act erratic. I also told the class that I had read old articles from prior bear markets, and it is impossible to calculate the value of stocks because future expectations for declining revenue growth mess up valuation equation inputs. The only real failsafe at market tops and bottoms is sentiment. By reading the newspapers, talking with people, listening to the media, all these things can help form that opinion. Since the class is more focused on math, the professor acknowledged my fringe views but disagreed about the math being broken.

**Friday, November 21, 2008**

**S&P 500:** 800.0

Every day, another bad news story. Rather than deflation hitting the headlines, investors are now concerned about inflation from quantitative easing. There is major concern about the money supply expanding too fast. Over the past month, every single asset class has been sold off, but gold is making a nice comeback. This is interesting because in classical market crashes, gold acts inversely to stocks. I'm witnessing old lessons reappear.

I attended a symposium on the current crisis with luminaries such as Alan Blinder speaking. Blinder spoke about the current crisis being fundamentals mixed with panic. He thinks a serious recession might occur, but the public and private sectors will need to work together and form a solution. What strikes me about all these "experts" – at Princeton and in the media – is that nobody knows where the markets are headed. Technically, if rates go to zero then price-to-earnings ratios should be infinite… however, only in extreme deflationary periods can rates go that low without triggering major inflation.

### Wednesday, November 26, 2008

**S&P 500:** 887.7

Quantitative easing has started to come up more often since the Fed announced the program. We had a healthy debate in class about it. A professor spoke about his time living in Japan during the early 1990s. It was not apparent what was about to transpire for most of the decade. He said that where Japan went wrong was keeping "zombie" institutions like banks alive rather than cleaning up the mess. He thinks Timothy Geithner is doing a great job moving forward quickly with action.

### Friday, November 28, 2008

**S&P 500:** 896.2

Black Friday. I'm at my grandmother's house outside Virginia celebrating Thanksgiving. As I look around the area, it's hard to reconcile the barrage of negative market news against reality. The mall was packed this morning. I presume areas around the country where houses were used as piggy banks are going through tougher times. Most people under the age of sixty only know short multi-month recessions, so spending should continue unless the recession gets deeper. Plenty of people remain employed – CNBC likes to turn the statistic around and say that roughly 95% of Americans are employed.

...

The S&P 500 closed around 900 during shortened trading. It has sunk below it, but quickly rallies back up. The market has held up remarkably well around this level and I have begun buying a small portion of index funds. I will continue to buy every other Friday.

# November 2008 Summary

- There is no consensus over how bad the economy will get, but the government has reacted quickly and forcefully with TARP, QE, and a few other programs. The current chaos is slowly bleeding into the real world. The unemployment rate catapults over 6%.

- Consumer spending plunges in large parts of the country, and the economy officially starts to contract. Princeton professors worry if we are entering a recession or going straight to depression.

- No amount of positive news flow can prevent the markets from cratering. The negative sentiment is so massive this month that any rally is short lived.

# Chapter 5

# December 2008: Darkness before Dawn

**Monday, December 1, 2008**

**S&P 500:** 816.2

The stock market collapsed over 9% today!!! A single day. That's historic by many measures. Typically, that type of repricing can take a full year to occur. The main reason for the selloff was the National Bureau of Economic Research declaring that the country has been in recession since December 2007. I tuned into CNBC during the lunch hour, and people kept harping on all the shenanigans Wall Street pulled to get Middle America into this mess. As CNBC ratings have increased, I think the average person watches this, gets scared, and sells even more of their stock portfolio.

...

I want to describe today, but a description will never substitute the experience. It's similar to taking an amazing photo of a landscape, but unable to capture the smell, the sun, and the sound. The selloff began as a snowball and later became an avalanche later in the afternoon. There was no positive energy or mood in the markets. The only direction was down. Word got out in the afternoon that many large hedge funds are putting up gates because so many investors want to rush to the exists. People were very scared on business shows today. Twitter was going crazy with doom and gloom. Not a single bull was brave enough to come forward. After the market closed, there were stories of grown men crying on the New York Stock Exchange trading floor. This was an extremely rare day. I have never seen something like it before, and it's easily the worst trading day I've ever witnessed. It really shows what can happen to markets. CNBC reported that it was the sixth worst trading day on record. It feels worse than October 15 because the back then there was a lot more chaos and confusion.

A crash made sense. This selloff felt more like an earthquake than an aftershock, and the start of fresh lows.

**Friday, December 5, 2008**

**S&P 500:** 876.1

I spoke with B about logistics for my upcoming winter break. I plan to work for a week and attend the hedge fund's annual holiday dinner. The venue this year will be a famous Michelin restaurant in the Time Warner Center. As I've written in the past, B runs a market-neutral fund, and the performance this year is flat because shorts and longs have canceled each other out. It's perfect neutrality. Many long/short hedge funds are down 30-50%, which I would argue means many of these hedge funds are not really funds but gambling vehicles. The outlook for the markets is weak, and B is quite negative on what will happen. He is convinced a lot of the selling is panic selling, which could get worse before it gets better.

**Friday, December 12, 2008**

**S&P 500:** 879.7

Large news came out the past couple days about a massive Ponzi scheme from a man named Bernie Madoff. I have never heard of this guy, and neither have most in the business media. B told me in the late 1990s several family offices chose to invest in Madoff instead of his mutual fund because Madoff promised 1%/month returns. Reportedly, actor Kevin Bacon had most of his money with Madoff. During deep market downturns, Ponzi schemes are revealed. This happened in the early 1930s. There is a great Reuters article on some of the Madoff news:

> The $50 billion allegedly lost would make the hedge fund one of the biggest frauds in history. When former energy trading giant Enron filed for bankruptcy in 2001, one of the largest at the time, it had $63.4 billion in assets.[8]

Markets continued to move around today. Volatility, however, is definitely coming down from the October-November months but still elevated in the mid-40s.

---

[8] https://www.reuters.com/article/us-madoff-arrest/bernard-madoff-arrested-over-alleged-50-billion-fraud-idUSTRE4BA7IK20081212

## Monday, December 15, 2008

**S&P 500:** 868.6

The thing about markets that really fascinates me isn't the money that can be made, but the idea that I get to witness the political and business events play out like a giant game of chess and make educated bets on future events. As John Maynard Keynes once said, "Successful investing is anticipating the anticipations of others." Despite all sorts of panic, the markets feel like they are holding around the 900 line. Frankly, this is a lot better than what occurred during the Great Depression. The equity market consolidating in this range is a huge positive. Credit markets have also healed from October. LQD, the main investment grade ETF, sits very close to $100/share. I generally think of LQD as a gigantic amalgamated bond. Credit trades at 100c on the dollar, so when LQD got to $85 a few months ago, it meant that very strong companies had debt trading at 85c on the dollar. Investment grade credit, in principle, should not sway much from the 100c baseline.

### Wednesday, December 17, 2008

**S&P 500:** 904.4

On my way up to New York to work with B, I overheard an interesting conversation on the train. A research analyst at JPMorgan was speaking on the phone about the semi-conductor space. He mentioned that Intel had ships loaded with processors at California ports. No demand meant that these containers were waiting offshore and in the port. Intel's stock is down about 40% this year, matching the Nasdaq. In high school, I was taught about the Great Depression featuring an unusual glut of basic household goods that had to be marked down. This Intel comparison sounds eerily similar.

### Friday, December 19, 2008

**S&P 500:** 887.9

CNBC had a segment about the auto makers today. The CEO of Chrysler stated that if his company goes bankrupt, it will spark a depression. This isn't the first time a CEO has tried to scare the general public. I was taught by B last summer to always ask "What is his/her motivation?" when something appears in the media. Whether it's a New York Times reporter or a CNBC guest, everyone has a motivation for saying something. Bob Nardelli, CEO of Chrysler, has been vocal about the need for some type of bailout of his company. Car sales are tanking as the economy falls. I understand his view that car manufacturing is a source of national pride and national security. The US government will nationalize industries that matter. My view is that if Chrysler has important technology, the US government will not let it go under. I disagree with Nardelli's extreme views. He was a colorful leader of Home Depot who gained a lot of notoriety a few years ago.

**Wednesday, December 24, 2008**

**S&P 500:** 868.2

Remember those cafeteria people back in September who I mentioned? Before going away on winter break, I asked about the economy. Every chef, server, and cashier were aware of the ongoing recession.

I returned to Florida a few days ago, and all my friends are talking about the recession, but most think it's temporary. No one has even heard of Goldman Sachs down here, and I love it. The distance from Wall Street is very healthy. It's like a different world. Also, the weather is way better: sunny and warm.

**Wednesday, December 31, 2008**

**S&P 500:** 903.3

What a year!!! The S&P 500 closed a little over 900. Considering the financial tsunami that rocked America back in the fall, I think this is a positive outcome. There is no question that the US is gripped by the worst business contraction since the 1930s. Here's where the markets ended the year: the Dow dropped 35%, the S&P 500 dropped 40%, and Nasdaq dropped 42%. I have to go back to the 1930s to see these types of annual figures!

I have a feeling that once people stop trying to call tops and bottoms, then the market will form a gentle base. I'd like to see exhaustion and mental defeat on the stock market's future direction. We are getting close, but not there yet. Nevertheless, I have continued buying small amounts of shares every Friday. If the bottom holds around 900 on the S&P 500, then it's the buy of a lifetime.

# December 2008 Summary

- In an historic move, the Federal Reserve lowers rates to zero. This has never happened in the post-WWII era. A deflationary environment emerges for the first time in living memory.

- A quiet acceptance of the current financial crisis takes over. The government's actions do little to change sentiment about the economy and risk assets. The overall mood is weak.

- Markets no longer appear in freefall but remain volatile. The S&P 500 has repeatedly hit the low 700s only to rally back to 900. The bond market has recovered from the crazy low levels of October.

- Paul Krugman calls the current slump the "Great Recession."

# Chapter 6

# January · February · March 2009: The Triple Whammy

**Monday, January 5, 2009**

**S&P 500:** 927.5

An interesting news item came out today about Research in Motion (RIMM) and their BlackBerry product line. As Wall Street has laid off professionals in their 30s and 40s, many of these folks are too afraid to share this news with their family. After getting a pink slip, they head to the nearest Verizon Wireless or AT&T store for a BlackBerry.

In other news, the markets have moved higher since last year and most traders on the NYSE are hopeful that the worst is behind us. Many companies right now are cutting numbers and announcing layoffs. A lot of this reflects a brutal Q4 2008. Judging from the market reaction, investors already have discounted a lot of these pre-announcements and bad news. The 900 level still remains solid support for the market after months of punishing news.

**Thursday, January 15, 2009**

**S&P 500:** 843.7

According to Bloomberg, the average S&P 500 target is about 1,050 at the end of 2009. That's 25% higher than where the market sits today. There may be some disconnect. The big talk of the day is how the depth of the recession may be worse than any professional forecast. Instead of traditionally lasting a few quarters, the contraction is actually accelerating. Dismal retail sales and an onslaught of layoff announcements continue to make major headlines. The selling pressure is very strong. I think it's clear right now that without the Treasury Department and Federal Reserve, the banking sector would be obliterated.

In times like these, I'm always curious what legendary investors are saying. Fortunately, Jack Bogle from Vanguard wrote a great article in the WSJ a week ago. He spoke about old lessons from the past.[9]

Below are the six lessons he reiterated:

- Beware of market forecasts, even by experts.
- Never underrate the importance of asset allocation.
- Mutual funds with superior performance records often falter.
- Owning the market remains the strategy of choice.
- Look before you leap into alternative asset classes.
- Beware of financial innovation.

---

[9] https://www.wsj.com/articles/SB123137479520962869

**Tuesday, January 27, 2009**

**S&P 500:** 845.7

Everyone in my classes knows how vocal I have been about stocks during this historic bear market. For months I've been captivated by the unfolding drama. I religiously checked stock quotes during classes and brought up any breaking news as the hours progressed. I am the "go to" guy for letting people know the temperature of the S&P 500. Just as fate would have it, a classmate of mine recently took a course last fall with New York Times writer Peter Appelbome. He is writing an article about Princeton students and their aspirations to work on Wall Street and wanted to speak with me. During my conversation with Appelbome, he said he wouldn't promise if I would be quoted in the article. He also emphasized I won't know the synopsis of his article until it's published. Regardless, I answered his questions. Crossing fingers that I make it.

In other news, this entire month can be described as "peaceful selling." Yes, there is awful news. It does feel priced in, and I think a bottom has formed. Markets may bob up and down, but this isn't the first time that I have felt the 800-900 line seems solid. While the recession continues, the stock market doesn't make the same type of headlines that it did late last year. Until the market rises above a nice round number like 1,000, it's not out of the woods yet.

### Thursday, February 5, 2009

**S&P 500:** 845.9

I just received a call that I will be in Saturday's paper. Peter Appelbome plans to quote me as a person skeptical that investment banking will come roaring back. In fact, he understands my viewpoint that the next decade will see other areas capture the imagination of would-be "Masters of the Universe." I don't think it will be Wall Street.

...

The volatility index remains in the 40s, but has risen slightly from last month. I've always been fascinated by that index. Whenever markets drop, volatility spikes. It's rarely the other way around. If I look at the chart, the true carnage was in October and November. This doesn't mean markets can't fall further. In fact, the markets seem to be selling off quite regularly over the past couple weeks. In the world of technical analysis, there is a term called a double bottom. A double bottom occurs when an asset sells off quickly and makes a decisive low. The asset then forms a small base and rallies over a several week or several month period before rolling over and staying in a depressed zone for a longer time. A double bottom can be seen as a turning point to be bullish because it flushes out the early, savvier investors as well as the speculative guys. The S&P 500 has formed a double bottom based on the chart. A quick, short ride to the 800-900 zone followed by a brief rally in late December and now an extended period of selling to the 800 area. If the markets can hold this ground, then it could mark the end of this bear. The beautiful thing about bear markets is that they are much shorter than bull markets and bottom when the future looks depressing.

**Friday, February 13, 2009**

**S&P 500:** 826.8

Tens of thousands of people read Applebome's New York Times article, including some folks at CNBC. I received an email inviting me to be on their show On the Money. This show profiles interesting stories related to business and finance every weeknight. I declined the invitation because the article's spotlight shouldn't be on me. Millions of Americans have lost their jobs, and I don't want to become a target.

...

In other news, John Taylor, who famously created the Taylor rule, wrote in the Wall Street Journal a scathing article about the US government for causing the current crisis. As he views it, the government incorrectly viewed the unfolding crisis in the mortgage market as one of liquidity rather than counterparty risk. It gets more complicated than this, however. He shows several instances leading up to the September 2008 crash where the government introduced mistaken policies rather than rigorously examining potential policy responses. As a result, the markets are sitting near 12-year lows. He ends the article with the following quote: "Massive responses with little explanation will probably make things worse. That is the lesson from this crisis so far."[10]

---

[10] https://www.wsj.com/articles/SB123414310280561945

**Monday, February 23, 2009**

**S&P 500:** 743.3

If there's a single song to remember this era by, it will be "Dead And Gone" by Justin Timberlake and T.I. The lyrics to the song are super relevant today. Timberlake sings "the old me, is dead and gone, dead and gone"… In some ways, that feels like the bull market from 2007. I've probably heard this song a dozen times a week since January. The beat is incredible, and really complements the mood of the markets. The entire world feels so different than when I entered Princeton in 2006. It's like a nuclear bomb went off in the stock market. 743 brings the S&P 500 back to 1996 and 1997 levels.

Politicians continue to bicker and debate on major news outlets about the current economy. There are rumors about cash leaving money markets. The mighty US government has the world's strongest and most professional military on earth but can't seem to halt a financial implosion. The economy is getting worse. Worse than anyone thought last year. There is confusion on CNBC about why the market broke below 800 after holding so strongly over the past five months. If things did get out of hand, the stock markets could just close I've heard. How right John Maynard Keynes was! Years ago, he said "the market can stay irrational longer than you can stay solvent."

…

I've asked classmates if they are concerned, but that makes them edgy. Putting on a brave and optimistic face about the situation appears to be what most are trying to do. I've accepted that we are born at a certain time and don't have complete control of where society and reality land at any given moment. If I graduate into a depression, so be it.

**Friday, February 27, 2009**

**S&P 500:** 735.1

Bonds officially beat stocks. At this point in time, it would have been better to buy bonds in the 1970s than stocks. It's unreal. I was taught that stocks beat bonds over the long run. Well, not anymore. If this deflationary mindset continues, the S&P 500 may indeed get to the 450 number that a professor mentioned last October. I still can't believe I'm even writing that in this entry. The S&P 500's next major support level is from 1994, when it sat around 450. That sounds insane, but it did happen in the 1929-1932 period. Anything is possible.

In other news, the cafeteria's brown sugar vendor went bankrupt. There will be no more brown sugar in my morning oatmeal until a new vendor's shipment arrives. If I had to think about it, this is the first and only sign that things are bad out there from inside the Princeton bubble.

**Tuesday, March 3, 2009**

**S&P 500:** 696.3

To me, this recent dip feels like a stock panic; a regime change. Not a bear market. Instead, it's a very, very acute drawdown that has taken the market below any reasonable level. 1929 and 1907 could be defined as stock panics. There hasn't been a similar period since that. 1987, while a crash, was more technical in nature and unrelated to an economic contraction. 2009 now feels like a stock panic wrapped into a bear market. Pundits on CNBC and Bloomberg are scratching their heads about the next leg down. I can only prophesize that some of the people who bought last fall are now being flushed out. There are several reasons people might be selling, but I'd wager that most sellers today are afraid of a protracted recession. The recent selloff is pushing more people to the exits.

...

A professor showed us a historical chart from work he did during the Japanese crash in the early 1990s. He placed valuation metrics over certain portions of the same timeline. Based on where the Nikkei 225 bottomed, the S&P 500 might bottom at 550. Japan has not confronted the issue of "zombie banks" from the 1980s that have soured loans. These banks continue to limp along without cleaning up their balance sheets. The professor stressed the importance of programs like TARP and QE, and how it could alter the trajectory of the S&P 500.

**Wednesday, March 11, 2009**

**S&P 500:** 721.4

What a doozy! The markets have bounced quite hard since last week. I haven't heard or read anyone who trusts this major rally. If there is a time that truly feels like there is "blood on the streets," then it's the past couple months. We seem to drift down slowly, and this can be psychologically taxing at times. These last couple months just seem to coalesce into one slow drawdown.

### Thursday, March 26, 2009

**S&P 500:** 832.9

Since the low of 666, the common voice from business news is that we are in a bear market rally. It feels like yesterday's news, though. So many people are beating the drum for lower lowers. Some think that by the summer we could see 500 on the S&P 500. When I spoke with people last fall and winter, people were mixed. As this market calamity has dragged on, nobody feels positive anymore. In fact, a lot of people are leaving equities altogether. My close friend J sold all of his holdings last month (he held IBM for life) and never plans to return to the market ever again.

Quantitative easing started last fall, but so far, the impacts appear minimal. This came out with large fanfare last year but has rarely been mentioned by business news this year.

# January · February · March 2009 Summary

- The short-term resurgence from the end of December to mid-January later proves to be a "dead cat bounce" as the 800-900 range on the S&P 500 gets taken out.

- While the market mayhem of late 2008 is over, the markets begin a quiet leg down through January and February. The relief rally from mid-March onward is greeted with suspicion by market participants. Relief rallies can turn out to be "dead cat bounces" or the start of the beginning of a new, beautiful bull market. It will be many months until the mid-March relief rally can be deemed either one.

- The classic notion that stocks beat bonds over long periods is destroyed. Over the prior 40 years (Feb. 1969 – Feb. 2009), bond returns officially beat total stock market returns by a slim margin.

- All bulls have been slaughtered. The career risk for making a case to own equities is too great. Even the Wall Street Journal shifts away from classic permabull status.

# Chapter 7

# April 2009 · May 2009: Aftermath

**Friday, April 3, 2009**

**S&P 500:** 842.5

These are lean times. It feels like a hurricane hit and left a path of destruction behind it. The stock market has long moved away from frontpage news during the heady days of October and November last year, but the economy remains very weak. The financial meltdown from last year has placed many people into idleness. The technology is better than a decade ago. The people are smarter than a decade ago. But, the stock market is back to a decade ago. The Shiller PE ratio is around 15. It hasn't been to this level since the 1980s. For most of the past two decades, it's fluctuated between 20 and 40.

...

Restaurants around Princeton University's campus are fairly empty for this time of year. I ate with my good friends D and J at Mediterra. The general manager said business is down by 20-30% from twelve months ago. We were stunned. After dinner, we walked around campus and debated the reality of a smaller economy. We postulated a few things. People want growth. People want to take risks. I'm a bit surprised that the average person is so negative on the stock market and economy despite improvements in technology since the mid-1990s. Asset prices may stay cheap for a while, but growth will undoubtedly return in the next five years. Stocks may even race back faster than anyone expects once quantitative easing takes effect.

**Friday, April 17, 2009**

**S&P 500:** 869.6

I spent the entire day at the New York International Auto Show. The exhibition had two types of vendors: OEMs (Ford, GM, BMW, etc.) and third-party merchants. The section with third-party vendors was nearly empty. I'd say one in four vendors from 2008. If this is the "new normal," yikes. I don't see how a smaller economy can function properly. The market got back to mid-1990s levels last month, despite the population increasing 50 million people during the same period. Anyway, I spoke with several people at Ford and GM, and they all said that they have never seen car discounts this extreme. The GM guy kept reciting the three core car brands going forward: BPG (Buick, Pontiac, GMC).

...

On my way back to Princeton Junction, one of the ticket clippers on NJ Transit talked to me about the economy. He has seen a fall in ridership. I asked him about the stock market and whether he looks at it or not. He mentioned he was thinking of buying some stocks the other day because, as he saw it, "some people during the Great Depression were buying stocks."

The S&P 500 has been bobbing up and down around 850-900 over the past several weeks. Last fall, that range felt like a firm bottom until March 9 happened. I don't know if we are seeing the bottom, but sentiment sure is damn weak out there. Even George Soros is uncertain about the validity of the recent March low.[11]

**Tuesday, April 28, 2009**

**S&P 500:** 855.2

On Bloomberg Radio this morning, I heard the term "green shoots" several times. Since around mid-April, it has become a popular phrase. For whatever reason, it's been used by so many people – politicians, talking heads, and professors. The term has really spread like wildfire. It goes hand in hand with guests stating that the economic contraction's second derivative (change in the rate of change) is now positive, which in plain English means that the economy's deceleration is slowing. There is no clear view on when the economy will bottom, but the news has markedly improved from just a month ago.

Several prominent investors, such as Warren Buffett and Paul Tudor Jones, have mentioned that the carnage we have witnessed during the past six months is way worse than the 2001 recession

---

[11] https://money.cnn.com/2009/04/07/markets/stockswatch/index.htm

and early 90s recession. Buffett thinks that we would need to go back to the 1930s to see something similar. Until this period, the stock market crash of the early 1970s was the most notable market correction for him.

**Monday, May 11, 2009**

**S&P 500:** 909.2

The S&P 500 has finally closed above 900!

Based on what I've experienced so far, let me put it into writing. Here we go: The news leading into a recession goes from bad to worse. Mainstream media amplifies this negativity. The markets tank, and the general public get scared. More selling unfolds. At some point, the market attempts to find a bottom, and then has a rally. This rally becomes a dead cat bounce as scared investors try to sell for a slightly smaller loss. A second bottom forms over a longer period (months instead of weeks). Eventually, the bad news ebbs but people remain very bearish. The markets quickly adjust upwards to prepare for the start of a new business cycle as brave and anonymous investors see value. It's impossible to know when valuations bottom. That's only possible to know in hindsight because earnings forecasts shift frequently during a recession.

People on CNBC and Bloomberg are split on whether March 9, 2009 was the firm bottom. There is no clear consensus Volatility, however, has been coming down and market news is starting to turn from negative to mellow. I'm not ready to say there is a bottom. The situation remains tenuous. 150 days of carnage so far.

**Friday, May 22, 2009**

**S&P 500:** 887.0

Author's Note: March 9, 2009 later held as the final bottom of the 2008-2009 bear market. During the months after March, many business and finance news commentators remarked that a bear market rally had begun, and lower lows would likely occur by the end of 2009. A "dead cat bounce" lasts days or weeks, but a bear market rally can last months. This, in fact, did not occur, and quantitative easing's full effects dispersed across financial markets throughout the year. Purchasers of sovereign debt moved to credit; purchasers of credit moved to preferred shares; purchasers of preferred shares moved to equities. The Federal Reserve continued swelling its balance sheet for the next several years via three iterations of quantitative easing, thereby shifting everyone up the risk curve. Without quantitative easing, it's likely that the markets would have gone much lower. The entries below will be the final one published for this book.

...

Markets can sometimes be echo chambers. There are many times when cratering markets feel like the end of the world. The best solution is to step outside and get fresh air. Thankfully, most people do not spend their days obsessing over market movements.

...

The markets are at an interesting inflection point. Do they continue to trend up? Or, come crashing down? Throughout my junior year, I have witnessed the five stages of grief. While fundamentals are awful, sentiment and emotions have been the driving force for acute market movements. No one knows where markets will land, but the negativity around owning equities is so extreme right now I have a hunch markets may have bottomed in March. The 900 level on the S&P 500 was very solid, and I bet that people buying in the fall didn't get the bounce they were expecting.

Those buyers turned into sellers in February and early March. At this point, everyone who could have sold stocks already did. There is now only one way to go: up.

# Conclusion

# Wisdom from a Bear Market

**Take Your Time Buying Shares**

While the markets didn't bottom until March 2009, "capitulation selling" occurred multiple times in November and December. There was no high volume, selling climax during this market crash. Yes, there were plenty of high volume +/- 10% days in the market, but these were part of the broader bear market.

Instead, the bottom occurred after a protracted drawdown that started in mid-January and continued through the beginning of March. The S&P 500 bottomed on March 9, 2009, at 666 during a depressing winter day in Princeton. I remember the late Mark

Haines, a prominent CNBC host, stating that March 9 felt like the bottom. To this day, I respect his judgement call. Just one week prior, a Princeton professor had warned about another 50% collapse in the market.

I recommend staggering purchases of shares every week during a bear market. You won't have to stress about being too large or "going down with the ship" as the markets find a bottom. Markets traditionally make major bottoms once the economic contraction slows or ends – two critical points that are hard to predict. Contractions don't last forever, but they can be psychologically scarring. The employment rate and economic wellbeing take much longer to heal, but by the time things are normal, markets have already recovered.

### "Money On The Sidelines" Won't Save You

During much of late 2008, so many folks came on CNBC and Bloomberg to discuss the large buckets of money from private equity firms waiting to invest.

Don't be deceived by this common phrase. Money on the sidelines never acts as a floor. Markets can fall fast, hard, and without care. It happened in 2008, as well as in 2001, 1972, 1929, and 1907.

## Popular Ideas Can Be Wrong

A lot of things were "supposed" to happen because of government programs and quantitative easing. Hyperinflation didn't occur, gold didn't replace the dollar, and anarchy didn't reign. All too often, so-called "experts" appeared on CNBC and Bloomberg with fantasies about financial Armageddon. Advancements have been made in monetary transmission and fiscal policies since 1907, 1929, and 2000. The best advice is to discount radical ideas (but be aware of them) and believe that a moderate outcome will prevail. The overwhelming fear by March 2009 drove asset prices to a generational low.

## Investor Rationality Is The Exception

The general public never buys low and sells high; in fact, they do the opposite. The 2008 crisis reinforced so many timeless investment lessons. Investors did not act rationally. Overly pessimistic scenarios played out wildly in the media. Both professional and amateur investors created a market tsunami. Very few understood that markets are discounting mechanisms. Sentiment provided an amazing opportunity for the enterprising investor to buy America on the cheap. As the S&P 500 tumbled in early 2009, low prices all but guaranteed healthy future returns. The very nature of human emotions has created buying opportunities in markets for several generations.

**Have Courage**

At the end of the day, markets are a game of wits. Be patient, have conviction, and avoid groupthink. When courage and beliefs are stronger than fear, beautiful investing happens.

# S&P 500 Largest Percentage Changes[12]

### Largest Daily Percentage Gains

|   | Date | Close | % Change |
|---|------|-------|----------|
| 1 | March 15, 1933 | 6.81 | +16.61 |
| 2 | October 30, 1929 | 22.99 | +12.53 |
| 3 | October 6, 1931 | 9.91 | +12.36 |
| 4 | September 21, 1932 | 8.52 | +11.81 |
| 5 | **October 13, 2008** | **1,003.35** | **+11.58** |
| 6 | **October 28, 2008** | **940.51** | **+10.79** |
| 7 | September 5, 1939 | 12.64 | +9.63 |
| 8 | April 20, 1933 | 7.82 | +9.52 |
| 9 | October 21, 1987 | 258.38 | +9.10 |
| 10 | November 14, 1929 | 19.24 | +8.95 |

---

[12] https://us.spindices.com/indexology/djia-and-sp-500/sizzlers-and-fizzlers

## Largest Daily Percentage Losses

|    | Date               | Close    | % Change |
|----|--------------------|----------|----------|
| 1  | October 19, 1987   | 224.84   | −20.47   |
| 2  | October 28, 1929   | 22.74    | −12.34   |
| 3  | October 29, 1929   | 20.43    | −10.16   |
| 4  | November 6, 1929   | 20.61    | −9.92    |
| 5  | October 18, 1937   | 10.76    | −9.27    |
| 6  | **October 15, 2008** | **907.84** | **−9.04** |
| 7  | **December 1, 2008** | **816.21** | **−8.93** |
| 8  | July 20, 1933      | 10.57    | −8.88    |
| 9  | **September 29, 2008** | **1,106.39** | **−8.79** |
| 10 | July 21, 1933      | 9.65     | −8.70    |

www.ingramcontent.com/pod-product-compliance
Lightning Source LLC
Chambersburg PA
CBHW020447220526
45464CB00002B/899